Dolly!

THE STORY OF
DOLLY PARTON
AND HER BIG DREAM

by
ROBYN McGRATH

Illustrated by
ELLEN SURREY

Christy Ottaviano Books

LITTLE, BROWN AND COMPANY
NEW YORK BOSTON

For Finley and Brendan, never stop dreaming. —RM

For Elzė and Emil, may all your big dreams come true. —ES

About This Book

The illustrations for this book were done in gouache. This book was edited by Christy Ottaviano and designed by Sasha Illingworth and Patrick Hulse. The production was supervised by Lillian Sun, and the production editor was Marisa Finkelstein. The text was set in Archer, and the display type is Nexa Rust.

Find out who you are and do it on purpose.
—Dolly Parton

*D*eep in a holler of the Great Smoky Mountains,
Dolly stood on her front porch, ready to perform.

She had a microphone for singing
and a guitar for strumming.

In her mind, she was all sparkles
and rhinestones.

As the fourth of twelve children, Dolly
was determined to be seen and heard.

She wrangled her siblings into being her audience.

And when they wouldn't, the chickens, pigs, and ducks would have to do.

From the get-go, Dolly linked up rhyming words and simple tunes to show her feelings. She tapped a rhythm when Mama snapped beans.

She clapped a beat when the geese honked overhead.

And when she was just five years old, she composed her first song about her handmade corncob doll, Tiny Tasseltop.

Dolly sang at home and in church.

With her grandpa as the local preacher, she belted out songs of praise and faith for the congregation.

Words flowed from Dolly's heart, loud and strong.

Each Saturday, Dolly's family crowded
around their battery-operated radio.

As Dolly listened to the Grand Ole Opry,
her heartbeat quickened,
she held her breath on each note,
and she felt the lyrics of joy and pain.

Dolly began to imitate the country greats, whose voices crooned into her living room—

Kitty Wells,

Patsy Cline,

and Johnny Cash.

She dreamed of herself onstage at the Opry.
Toe tapping,
knee slapping,
belting out country tunes.

But people said,
"You're just a kid."
And,
"Too young for the Opry."

Dolly stood tall. She believed she had something to say.

Living on a farm meant work for young Dolly.

She hoed corn and planted pumpkins, beans,
and turnips with her family.

But Dolly preferred to be back at the house,
    writing songs,
        singing songs,
           and most important—dreaming.

When the Parton family had time to sit a spell, they played some Appalachian porch pickin' music.

Guitars, banjos, and fiddles filled the holler with twangs of
love,
loss,
and longing.

Dolly would pick a little and play a lot.

She slapped the tambourine, plucked the banjo, and pounded the piano,
watching and learning from each member of her family.

It was Uncle Bill, on her mama's side, who began to take notice of Dolly's musical talent.

When Dolly received her first guitar, she learned some chords, and everyone saw how quick she made a lick of it.

Her music had cadence, harmony, and tempo! And that voice?

Sweet,

soulful,

and something fierce!

At school, some kids picked
on Dolly for being poor.

They laughed and mocked the clothes
her mama had sewn from scraps.

But Dolly wiped away the tears.

They couldn't stop her from dreaming.

She turned her hurt feelings into lyrics
and found a melody to match.

On winter nights, huddled by the warmth of the fire,
Mama sang songs and told stories of worlds far away.

Each note carried Dolly from her mountain home to Nashville.

Each note added kindling to her own growing flame.

Uncle Bill helped Dolly approach local millionaire Cas Walker, who broadcast a weekly variety show.

Her confidence and wide smile earned Dolly a radio and television gig.

With butterflies in her belly, she took the stage.

Hesitant at first, she sang higher and higher with pure joy and fell in love with the live audience.

Soon after, Dolly and her uncle started making trips to Nashville,
determined to get her a guest spot at the Opry.
They knocked on doors,
sent recordings to record companies,
and approached people who had musical connections.

But time and time again she was told,
        "You're just a kid."
And,
        "Too young for the Opry."

Dolly wouldn't take no for an answer.

She and her uncle spent countless nights
sleeping in the car with little gas money
to make the long trips back home.

Dolly would pluck a tune on her guitar or drum a rhythm on the dashboard.

Stories in verse flowed from her lips,
songs of home, family, love, and dreams.

Finally, Dolly's persistence paid off.

One night, another singer agreed to let Dolly go onstage in his place at the Grand Ole Opry!

Dolly's dreams had led her here.
To this moment.
To THIS stage.

And she was...
just a kid.

When it was time, Johnny Cash introduced Dolly.

"We've got a little girl here from up in East Tennessee. Her daddy's listening to the radio at home, and she's gonna be in real trouble if she doesn't sing tonight, so let's bring her out here."

Dolly walked to the mic in a daze.

She lifted her head to the lights, smiled bright, and "let 'er rip"!

She sang for everyone who had ever believed in her.

And Dolly's deep feelings sparked a connection.

The audience felt her energy,
          her emotion.

There were three encores that night!

Three!

Everyone wanted to hear more of Dolly.

          Dolly stoked the fire,
                    put pen to paper,
                              and continued to write her stories into songs.

The day after high school graduation, Dolly headed straight to Nashville.

She struggled to get a job, pay rent, and eat.

But Dolly continued to write and sing.
Sing and write.

Then Dolly earned a coveted spot on *The Porter Wagoner Show*, a popular weekly television program.

She wowed fans with her humor and vocals, and her songs flew to the top of the charts.

Dolly lifted people up with her voice,
transporting them to the Great Smoky Mountains,
        to her roots,
                and to her family.

With nails, hair, heels, sparkles, and that voice, always that
voice, she no longer had to wrangle an audience.

Dolly—finally seen and heard as the artist she was—
        had a real microphone for singing,
                a plethora of instruments for playing,
                        and no shortage of rhinestones.

And above all else, Dolly remained true to herself and her
dreams, letting her songs guide us home.

MORE ABOUT DOLLY

*D*olly Rebecca Parton was born in rural Appalachia on January 19, 1946. Growing up "dirt poor," in a one-room cabin with no electricity or running water, Dolly saw music as a way to channel her incredible vision, passion, and determination.

At a young age, Dolly learned to use her voice when classmates teased her. Ignoring their criticisms, she created music to express her feelings and keep focused on her dreams. Today she continues to use her wide smile, bubbly laughter, and humor to deflect a conversation. She will be the first to poke fun at herself.

There is no mistaking Dolly's signature look: beaded, sequined clothes, six-inch heels, acrylic nails, and at least 365 wigs—one for every day of the year! Dolly has never been afraid to stand out: "I feel glamorous on the inside, so I want to look it on the outside." Even her guitars share her signature sparkle and butterfly love.

During the course of her career, Dolly has won many awards, including nine Grammys and the National Medal of Arts. She was even nominated for two Academy Awards for her music. Dolly has written more than three thousand songs and has sung and recorded with numerous artists. While she is mostly known for her singing voice, Dolly can also play a multitude of instruments: the piano, banjo, fiddle, harmonica, dulcimer, guitar, and harp. She might play up to seven different instruments during a concert!

Writing and singing gave Dolly her start, but her commitment to literacy drives the mission of her Dollywood Foundation. Each year, the foundation provides scholarships to high school students in Sevier County, Dolly's childhood community. To date, the Imagination Library, started in honor of her father, has gifted more than 125 million books to children in need worldwide. Dolly believes in the potential of all children, as well as the importance of education and literacy as a means for a better tomorrow.

Fans of Dolly span generations and all walks of life. Her enormous heart can be felt in the words she writes and her charitable endeavors: literacy, health care, and marriage equality. The Dollywood Parks and Resorts alone have brought a great deal of jobs to Sevier County.

Yet despite her remarkable career as a singer, songwriter, actress, businesswoman, producer, and humanitarian, Dolly remains humble and authentic. Her generosity has become an inspiration for many. Never afraid to dream big, the country legend attributes her faith in God and daily prayer in guiding her dreams. And just when you think that would be enough—Dolly continues to dream more.

THE GRAND OLE OPRY

Starting in 1925 as a radio broadcast, the Grand Ole Opry has a rich history dedicated to honoring country music. Located in Nashville, Tennessee, the Opry has been a destination for hundreds of thousands of people to see live performances of some of country music's greatest talent. It has been called the "home of American music" and is credited with launching countless country music careers.

welcome to

NASHVILLE

DOLLYISMS

"If you see someone without a smile, give 'em yours."

"It's hard to be a diamond in a rhinestone world."

"The way I see it, if you want the rainbow, you got to put up with the rain."

"We cannot direct the wind, but we can adjust the sails."

*"I've always been misunderstood because of how I look.
Don't judge me by the cover 'cause I'm a real good book!"*

*"You need to really believe in what you've got to offer, what your talent is—
and if you believe, that gives you strength."*

"If you don't like the road you're walking, start paving another one."

"You'll never do a whole lot unless you're brave enough to try."

*"I believe in family, I believe in love, and I believe
that together we can change the world."*

SOURCES

Books

Miller, Stephen. *Smart Blonde.* London: Omnibus Press, 2008.

Nash, Alanna. *Dolly.* Los Angeles: Reed Books, 1978.

Parton, Dolly. *Dolly: My Life and Other Unfinished Business.* New York: HarperCollins, 1994.

Parton, Dolly. *Dream More.* New York: Penguin Group, 2012.

Schmidt, Randy L.. *Dolly on Dolly: Interviews and Encounters with Dolly Parton.* Chicago: Chicago Review Press Incorporated, 2017.

Websites

dollyparton.com

imaginationlibrary.com

dollywoodfoundation.com

Parton, Dolly, interview by Terry Gross. *Fresh Air*, NPR, September 6, 2010. https://www.npr.org/transcripts/129611133?storyId=129611133?storyId=129611133

Watts, Cindy. "Dolly Parton retraces steps from East Tennessee home to Opry circle." *The Tennessean.* October 4, 2019. https://www.tennessean.com/story/entertainment/music/country-mile/2019/10/04/dolly-parton-recalls-winding-road-her-native-sevier-county-opry/3849915002/